Mother's Day

Laura Pratt

Weigl

Published by Weigl Educational Publishers Limited
6325 10th Street S.E.
Calgary, Alberta
T2H 2Z9

www.weigl.com

Library and Archives Canada Cataloguing in Publication data available upon request.
Fax 403-233-7769 for the attention of the Publishing Records department.

ISBN: 978-1-77071-631-5 (hard cover)
ISBN: 978-1-77071-632-2 (soft cover)

Printed in the United States of America in North Mankato, Minnesota
1 2 3 4 5 6 7 8 9 0 14 13 12 11 10

062010
WEP230610

Editor: Josh Skapin
Design: Terry Paulhus

Weigl acknowledges Getty Images as its primary image supplier for this title.
iStock: page 5, 15, 17.

We gratefully acknowledge the financial support of the Government of Canada through the Canada Book Fund for our publishing activities.

Contents

What is Mother's Day?

Mother's Day is a day for celebrating mothers and honouring their hard work. On this day, children spend time with their mother. They might cook her a meal or give her a special gift.

Happy Mother's Day

5

When is Mother's Day?

In Canada, Mother's Day is celebrated on the second Sunday in May each year. Any woman who helps care for a child may be celebrated on Mother's Day. This can include aunts, grandmothers, stepmothers, or sisters.

Mother's Day History

People have been celebrating the hard work of mothers since ancient times. Ancient Greeks held a festival to honour Cybele. She was the mother of the Greek gods. The festival was held around the first day of **spring** each year. Ancient Romans had a holiday to honour a mother goddess named Juno. Mothers were often given gifts on this day.

Mothering Sunday

In the 1600s, Christians set aside a day to celebrate Mary. Mary was the mother of Jesus Christ. Later, the day became a time to honour all mothers. The day was known as Mothering Sunday. It took place on the fourth Sunday of Lent. Lent is the name given to the 40 days before Easter.

Mothers in Great Britain

In Great Britain, Mothering Sunday honours all mothers. In an early tradition, children would bake an almond "mothering cake" for their mother. They would also give her fresh flowers, such as **roses** or carnations. This tradition continues today.

Mother's Day for Peace

In the late 1800s, an American woman named Julia Ward Howe wanted women to take a stand against war. Soon, women across the United States took part in Mother's Day for **peace** events. This day was never made a formal holiday.

Modern Mother's Day

In the early 1900s, Anna Jarvis spent many years caring for her sick mother. After her mother died, Anna missed her. She thought there should be a special day for children to honour their mothers. The first Mother's Day celebration was held in 1908. It took place at the church where Anna's mother had taught. Soon, people across the United States and Canada were celebrating Mother's Day.

Happy Mother's Day

17

Mother's Day Traditions

Mothers often receive gifts and cards from their children on Mother's Day. Sometimes, children give their mother **crafts** they make at school. Many children enjoy making their mother breakfast.

19

Mother's Day Around the World

There are different kinds of Mother's Day celebrations around the world. Each country has its own traditions. In Scotland, mothers are honoured with carlings. Carlings are pancakes made of dried peas. In Thailand, Mother's Day is celebrated on the queen's birthday.

Symbols of Mother's Day

The white carnation is a symbol of Mother's Day. Anna Jarvis sent 500 white carnations to the first Mother's Day celebration at a church in West Virginia. Her mother's favourite flower was the white carnation.

23

Glossary

crafts	peace
roses	spring

Index